TOMORROW'S SCIENCE

Genetic Engineering

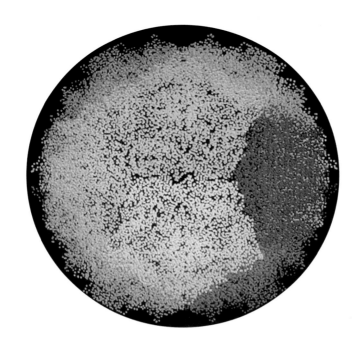

Anne Rooney

Chrysalis Education

TOMORROW'S SCIENCE

Artificial Intelligence
Genetic Engineering
Internet Technologies
Medicine Now

Distributed in the United States by

Smart Apple Media, 1980 Lookout Drive, North Mankato, Minnesota 56003

Copyright © Chrysalis Books PLC 2003

ISBN 1-59389-120-2

The Library of Congress control number 2003104917

Editorial manager	Joyce Bentley
Editor:	Susie Brooks
Designer:	John Jamieson
Consultant:	Helen Cameron
Picture researcher:	Aline Morley

Also thanks to: Gill Adams, Allan Bradley, Pip Hardy and Penny Worms

Anne Rooney asserts her moral right to be recognized as the author of this work.
If you have any comments on this book, please email her at anne@annerooney.co.uk.
For more information on her work, visit www.annerooney.co.uk.

Printed in Hong Kong

Picture acknowledgements

All reasonable efforts have been made to trace the relevant copyright holders of the images contained within this book. If we were unable to reach you, please contact Chrysalis Children's Books.

B = bottom; *L* = left; *R* = right; *T* = top

Cover (DNA) Digital Vision (embryo) SPL/James Stevenson **Background 4-48** Digital Vision **1** SPL/ M Hogle/ Harvard Medical School **4** Corbis/Reed Kaestner **5** SPL/Andrew Syred **6** Corbis/Archivo Icongrafico/S.A **7** SPL/Ed Young/Agstock **9** *L* SPL/Martin Dohrn *R* SPL/Dr Jurgen Scriba **10** Corbis/Francis G. Mayer **11** *L* Corbis/Royalty Free *R* (see 1) **12-13** Corbis/Royalty Free **14** Corbis/Hans Georg Roth **15** Corbis/Bettmann **16** Corbis/Sygma/Ellis Richard **17** Corbis/Jim Lake **18** The Kobal Collection/Columbia **19** Corbis/Bettmann **20** SPL/Simon Fraser/RVI, Newcastle upon Tyne **21** SPL/Will and Demi Mcintyre **22** Corbis/Curtis/P.A. News/Corbis KIPA **23** *T* (see cover) *B* SPL/James King-Holmes **24** SPL/Tracey Dominey **25** Rex **26-27** Corbis/Sygma **28** Corbis/Jose Luis Pelaez Inc **29** Corbis/Patrick Ward **30** SPL/Will and Demi Mcintyre **32** Corbis/Anthony Cooper/Ecoscene **34** Corbis/Adrian Arbib **35** Corbis/Lindsay Hebberd **36** SPL/Rudiger Lehnen **37** SPL/Sinclair Stammers **38** SPL/Mark Clarke **39 and 40** SPL **41** Still Pictures/Thomas Raupach **42** Still Pictures/B & C Alexander **43** *T* SPL/George Bernard *B* Corbis/Paul A. Souders **44** Corbis/Roger Ressmeyer **45** Corbis/Elio Ciol.

Contents

Genetics today

Have you ever wondered why you have blue eyes like your mom, or why your sister's hair is curly like your uncle's? Many of our features are determined by chemicals called genes, which we inherit from our parents and even grandparents. Scientists are learning more and more about this process, and with their growing knowledge comes the chance to control genetic features—not only in people but in other species, too.

In this book, we'll look at how people are beginning to work with genetic information, and think about some of the questions this new science raises. These are difficult but intriguing issues about what it's right and wrong to do. There may be no "right" answers, but they are issues we must think about if we're to play an active part as citizens and have a say in how our world develops.

This book won't tell you what to think. It will give you some scientific background and present many different views and possibilities. Then you can think about and discuss the issues, forming your own opinions—opinions that you are able to explain and defend.

Many of your physical features are inherited—that's why you share characteristics with other members of your natural family.

Genetics in action

All plants and animals have characteristics they inherit from their parents. What they look like and how they work are passed on from one generation to the next. Some features are fixed for the type of plant or animal—so all blackbirds have two legs and a beak, for example. But others vary between individuals—some spaniels are brown while others are white.

The "recipe" for an individual plant or animal is carried in its genes. This includes information for the features that are always the same and for those that differ between individuals. Genes are passed on from one generation to the next through the process of reproduction. A living thing starts as one cell, which divides again and again to form more cells. Each time a cell divides, its genes are copied into the new cells.

There's about 5 feet of DNA in each of your cells. If you laid all the DNA in your body end to end, it would reach to the sun and back about 40 times!

Definition: genes

Genes carry the information that your body needs to build all your cells. Each gene determines a single characteristic, such as eye color. You have about 30,000 different genes. They are strung together into chromosomes, which are molecules of the chemical DNA.

Chromosomes (shown highly magnified here) are arranged and inherited in pairs—one from each parent. Humans have 23 pairs of chromosomes in every cell.

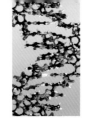

Genetics today
Working with genetics

We tend to think that working with genetic information is a new development, but this isn't actually true. We just didn't know we were doing it until quite recently.

Selective breeding

People have bred animals and plants to be how they want them to be for many centuries. So farmers would pick the sheep with the thickest wool and breed from them, perhaps eating the less woolly sheep. They would gather seed from the strongest wheat plants to sow for the next crop. Choosing to breed from particular individuals in this way is called selective breeding.

In the Middle Ages, hunting dogs were bred for their speed, strength, and ability to track animals. Although no one understood how selective breeding worked, they made use of it to produce the animals they wanted.

Decoding genetics

All our farm animals and crops have been developed through centuries of selective breeding. But we now understand that the characteristics we might want in a plant or animal are fixed by its genes. We're beginning to find out which genes control which features in some animals and plants.

DNA is made up from the same chemicals in all organisms, and the same groupings occur in many species. A quarter of a human's DNA is the same as that of a lettuce!

Genetic engineering

We can now work directly with genes, adding, removing, and modifying them to make the plants and animals we want. It's called genetic engineering. We can "cut and paste" genes within the chromosomes of a single species or even between species—taking a gene from a fish and putting it into a plant cell, for example. When the cell divides to make more cells, the changed DNA will be copied into the new cells.

"I don't see that nature has done such a good job that we can't improve on it."

FAY WELDON, 1997

Fact: upbringing

Not all your characteristics are coded in your genes. Some come about as a result of how you are brought up, where you live, the type of diet you eat, the experiences you've had, and so on. These are called environmental factors. You may have the genes to grow tall, for example, but if you are underfed it won't happen.

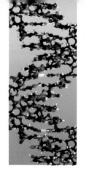

Genetics today
The Human Genome Project

Before we can work with individual genes, we need to know what they do. Learning what our own genes do has been the work of the Human Genome Project, which aims to find out the position and function of every one of the 30,000 human genes.

Mapping the genome

Finding out what each gene does is a long and complicated process. Scientists begin by cutting the chromosomes into chunks and using very sophisticated equipment to work out the order of groups of chemicals on these chunks. These mappings are then put back together, giving a list of genes on the chromosome in the order in which they appear.

A large amount of the DNA in a chromosome is known as "junk DNA". We don't know what it does, or if it does much at all. Junk DNA isn't mapped, but it is identified.

Finally, all the information collected is put into a large database, which has been made available to anyone who needs it, following the project's completion in 2003.

So what now?

Genetic knowledge will help us to:
- understand, prevent and cure many diseases
- find ways to help wounds heal more quickly
- understand how we evolved and how other species evolved
- understand the differences between people
- identify people from small samples of tissue—such as skin or blood.

Curing disease

The information we gain from the Human Genome Project will help us to understand how our bodies work. We will be able to say whether someone is likely to get a particular disease and to prevent or cure some inherited conditions.

Fact: DNA

You share 99.9 percent of your DNA with every other person on the planet. Less than a thousandth of your DNA carries the differences between you and everyone else.

8

Proving identity

We can already cross-match DNA from tiny samples of body tissue—such as hair, blood, or skin—with the DNA of a known person. This can help us to identify victims of war, disaster, or crime and prove whether people are related to one another.

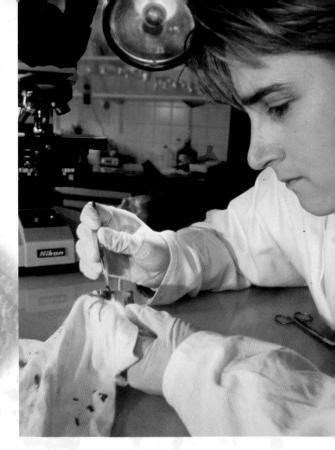

DNA "fingerprinting" may soon replace traditional fingerprints. A DNA sample could reveal the physical features of a criminal.

Even a tiny sample of blood, skin, or hair is enough for **DNA** testing to help us identify a criminal or victim.

Looking ahead

With the possibility of knowing almost anything about someone by studying their DNA, we face interesting and difficult questions about our own rights and what we should and shouldn't do. Are we entitled to keep our own genetic information secret? How will people be affected by knowing they are likely to develop a serious disease? Is it safe or right to make changes to the DNA of any species of plant or animal?

Who owns and can make money from genetic information? You will have the chance to explore these and other ethical issues as you work through this book.

Definition: ethics

Ethics is the study of what is right and wrong. Some people believe there is an absolute code of ethics—things "are" right or wrong. Others think that we make up our own ethical codes, which will be different in different societies.

What's it to you?

Why should you be concerned about progress in genetics? It may all seem too distant to matter to you—but you're involved more closely than you think. Advances made in all areas of science and technology affect each of us in some way or another. Here are a few general things to think about as you read the rest of this book.

In Christian tradition, Adam and Eve were forbidden by God to eat fruit from the Tree of Knowledge. Tasting the fruit—and discovering both good and evil—led to their banishment from paradise. Could knowledge really be our downfall?

Are we ready to do this?

Understanding genes will give us new powers. Will we be able to manage them? Can we be sure what we learn will be used only for good? And can we agree on what is "good?" We can't "unlearn" knowledge once we've learnt it. We need not only knowledge, but the wisdom to use it.

Are there dangers?

Many areas of research may hold risks of which we know nothing at the moment. If there's a chance things might go wrong, does it mean that we shouldn't experiment? Is it safe to work with something we don't fully understand? Who should decide?

In the 1930s, bad farming practices led to the destruction of vast areas of land in the U.S. Human actions have caused many disasters in the past. What could happen next?

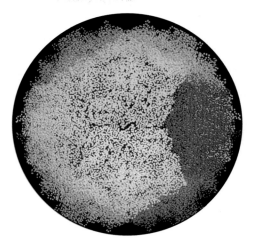

In 2002, scientists used an online "recipe" and genes bought by mail order to create a working polio virus. How can we stop people making viruses such as this one, which could threaten the world?

Who counts?

In many areas of life, we have to balance a benefit to a large number of people against a disadvantage to a small number of people. Genetics presents many problems of this type.

Suppose you were at risk of inheriting a genetic disorder. Doctors may put pressure on you to have tests or take part in studies to help them discover how the disease works, but you might not want to know if you had the condition. Your own interests would then be in conflict with the interests of society.

Who chooses?

Many choices in life lead to further questions. Say it is accepted that a couple may abort their baby if tests reveal it will be blind. Should a blind couple therefore be free to abort their baby if it isn't blind? How may each person justify their right to choose?

Over to you

We all have a right to be involved in decisions about the world's future. But in order to have the power to change things, we need to understand the issues that affect us all. You will need to be able to separate fact from opinion in the things you read and hear. You will need to be able to disentangle reliable information from media scare stories and public relations hype. If you can do this, and shape your own informed views, you will be able to play an important part in the changing world. Use the "Ask yourself" boxes in the following chapters as a starting point for discussing the issues raised.

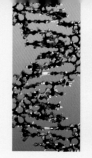

Whose genes are they anyway?

Genetic research is valuable—there is money to be made in finding out more about the human body and the natural world. But some people are becoming concerned about who may use this new knowledge, and for what. Can the natural properties of plants and animals be "owned" by anyone?

"I am determined not to steal and not to possess anything that should belong to others... I will prevent others from profiting from human suffering or the suffering of other species on Earth."

SECOND BUDDHIST PRECEPT, THICH NHAT HANH

Legal protection

In many countries, if you develop or invent something new you can apply for a patent to show that it's your invention and to stop other people copying it to make money. If you invented a new machine, for instance, it's clearly fair that you should be able to protect your idea. But now people are patenting genetic developments.

"Patents shall be available for any inventions, whether products or processes, in all fields of technology, provided that they are new, involve an inventive step and are capable of industrial application."

TRIPs (TRADE-RELATED ASPECTS OF INTELLECTUAL PROPERTY RIGHTS) AGREEMENT, MARRAKESH, 1994

Patenting plants

Plant breeders try to produce plants with the qualities that growers want. They may make roses with a good smell and long-lasting flowers, wheat that survives well in poor soil, or apple trees that have large crops of apples. To protect the money they have put into developing them, they apply for patents so that other people can't copy their plants. But plants produce seeds and these grow into new plants. It can be illegal to allow seeds to fall on the soil in your garden and grow by themselves.

Many plants carry labels saying they are patented. This means you can't take cuttings or grow new plants from the seeds without breaking the law.

Ask yourself

◆ Is a plant an invention, even if it is possible that the same plant could grow through chance pollination of two existing plants?
◆ Should it be possible to patent a plant, or any other living organism?

Whether or not you can take cuttings in your garden might seem rather unimportant. But the issue gets more complicated.

Whose genes are they anyway?

Local interests

The Convention on Biodiversity, which began at the Earth Summit in Rio de Janeiro in 1992, aims to protect species of plants and animals around the world. One of its terms says that local people should receive payments for products made from species that are native to their area. The U.S. has refused to accept this, but 180 countries have agreed to the terms. The payments are not being made. The United Nations says poor countries are losing billions of dollars a year through non-payment.

Case study

The plant ayahuasca has been used in medicine for centuries in Ecuador, South America. But the U.S.'s International Plant Medicine Corporation (IPMC) has now taken out a patent on it. The Ecuadorian people want IPMC to give up their patent. Should IPMC be allowed to make money from a plant they have researched and invested in? Should they be allowed to prevent others using the plant freely?

Ask yourself

◆ If we take a plant—and traditional knowledge—from an area and use it to make money, should we pay the people?
◆ Who should we pay? Their government? Or perhaps local individuals who work with the plant or share their knowledge?
◆ Who owns traditional knowledge?

U.S. businesses have patented new varieties of basmati rice developed from strains bred by Indian farmers. Their patent is not recognized in India, but if it were it would prevent farmers continuing their own breeding programs and making similar strains of rice.

Genes for sale

As we become able to cure more and more illnesses by working with genes, some people's genes are likely to become valuable. One example of this is the gene that produces sickle-cell anemia, a condition in which red blood cells are the wrong shape and make sufferers dangerously ill. This gene also gives people protection against malaria, so it could be useful in helping doctors to find a cure for or prevent malaria.

The village of Eyam in England cut itself off during a plague epidemic in the 17th century—no one was allowed to leave, in the hope of containing the disease and protecting people outside the village. Many people died, but some survived. Descendants of the survivors are more resistant to many diseases than most people. Their genes could be valuable.

Ask yourself

◆ If you have a gene that protects you against a disease, can you sell it?
◆ Should everyone with the same gene share in the payout?
◆ Or should you donate your genes to help humanity, even though the medical company using them will benefit?

A "gene treaty?"

Some scientists and politicians say there should be a "gene treaty" that makes all genetic information a shared resource for anyone in the world to use. This would prevent anyone patenting a gene, but companies could still patent medicines and other treatments. Decisions need to be made as to how this idea would be managed globally.

Your own genes

Your genes are unique to you—no one else in the world has exactly the same genetic make-up, unless you have an identical twin. But are they entirely yours? What rights do you have to your own genes? And what rights should anyone else have to them? As DNA testing becomes cheaper and quicker, it's getting easier to find out things about people. How much would you want anyone to know about you?

Politicians are among those whose jobs could be threatened by DNA testing. Should they have to hire people to collect cutlery, glasses, and napkins they've used so that no traces of their DNA can be "stolen?"

DNA everywhere

It's impossible to go through a single day without leaving bits of your DNA all over the place. There will be traces of saliva on the cups and cutlery you use, hairs left in combs or on the backs of chairs, flakes of skin in your clothes. You might think this doesn't really matter—why would anyone want to check up on your DNA anyway? But it might matter very much if you're a public figure.

Once genetic testing becomes widely available, we're likely to see all kinds of uses for it and many tests might be carried out without the consent or knowledge of the person being tested.

Unauthorised testing

We don't know which character traits are set by people's genes and which depend on upbringing. There may be genes for intelligence (and lack of it), for homosexuality, for creativity, for alcoholism, or for criminality. If this is the case, a person's genetic make-up could be important to people they become involved with, such as employers and partners. An employer could test hairs left on the back of a chair by an interviewee, to see if they're likely to fall ill or just turn out to be lazy. Or you might one day want to check that your future husband or wife isn't likely to develop depression or heart disease—or become an alcoholic. At the moment there's no law to stop you.

An organization in California is offering to copyright celebrities' DNA, showing how worried some people are about what could happen to 'stolen' DNA.

Case study

Ronald Reagan was US president from 1980 to 1988. In 1994, he announced that he had Alzheimer's disease— a condition which causes a person's brain to deteriorate so that they become totally dependent on other people. If we'd had genetic tests for Alzheimer's in 1980, a news reporter or opposition politician could have found out that he was at risk from the disease, and made this information public. Would Reagan ever have been elected president if people had known previously that he was likely to develop Alzheimer's?

Your own genes

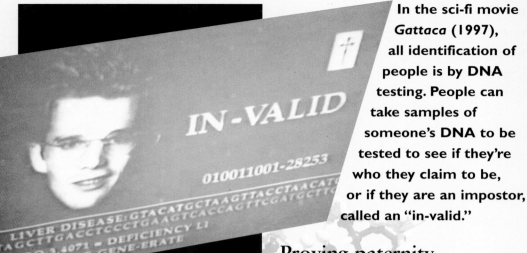

Proving paternity

Proving paternity – that someone is the father of a particular child – has long depended on DNA testing and can now be carried out secretly with "stolen" DNA samples. U.S. film producer Steven Bing was proven to be the father of a child after private detectives stole used dental floss from his garbage and had his DNA tested and compared with that of the child.

The Human Genetics Commission (which advises the U.K. government on issues raised by genetic research) is recommending a law to prevent the theft and examination of DNA.

Case study

The U.S. Burlington Northern and Santa Fe Railway Company was fined $2.2 million in 2001, after secretly carrying out a genetic test on its employees. The test was to check whether employees were particularly prone to RSI (repetitive strain injury)—a common industrial complaint. The company intended to fight compensation claims for RSI by showing the workers had a genetic tendency to develop it. The company was fined for discriminating against employees likely to develop RSI, not because the testing was carried out.

Ask yourself

◆ What rules should there be about who can take and test DNA samples?
◆ Does it matter what the test is for?
◆ Should the person being tested be entitled to know the results?

DNA tests and the law

In some countries, the police want to store DNA samples from criminals and even people they have questioned. This would mean they could quickly link a person to a crime—or show that someone was innocent of a crime—by comparing body tissues from a crime scene with DNA information in their database.

Governments concerned about immigration—people coming from other countries to live—use DNA tests to check claims that someone has a relative in the country they are entering.

Ask yourself

◆ Should everyone be made to provide a DNA sample to help fight crime?
◆ Could we stop the information being used for the wrong purposes, or falling into the wrong hands?
◆ Should there be rules about what is done with DNA samples, or knowledge that arises from them, in future years?

DNA after death

We never like to imagine we'll be killed in an accident, but if you were, a database of everyone's DNA would help the rescue services identify your body. The U.S. Army already has a database of the DNA of acting soldiers so that their bodies can be identified if they're killed in battle. How would you feel about giving a DNA sample for this purpose?

Chemical tests on Napoleon's hair in the 1990s tried to find out whether he died of cancer or poisoning. No real conclusion was drawn, but DNA testing could tell us a great deal about people who have died—including things that could not have been known when they lived. How would you feel about future generations testing bits of you like this?

Genes and disease

Until recently, people had babies not knowing if they'd be born healthy. But now we're often able to tell in advance, by carrying out genetic tests on the parents.

Dominant or recessive?

For every characteristic, we each have two genes—one inherited from each parent. Many genes take one of two forms: dominant or recessive. If one of a pair of genes is dominant, it will always be expressed—you'll have the characteristic that it determines. But a recessive gene will only be expressed if both genes in the pair are the same.

If one of your parents has a dominant gene for a genetic disorder, and the gene is passed on to you, you will develop the disorder. But if a disease depends on a recessive gene, you would need both parents to pass on that gene in order for it to be expressed.

Testing for abnormalities

There's already a genetic test for cystic fibrosis (CF), so parents can tell before conceiving whether either or both of them has one of the gene defects that cause CF. If they both have a CF gene (which is recessive), there is a one in four chance their child will have CF.

Cystic fibrosis is a genetic disease that affects the lungs and digestive system. Sufferers have a disrupted and uncomfortable life and are likely to die young.

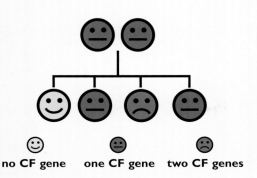

no CF gene   one CF gene   two CF genes

This diagram shows the statistical chances of a child inheriting a CF gene. In real life this will vary—so it's possible that out of four "at risk" children, none, some, or all will have CF.

Parents with a CF gene may choose:
◆ to use in vitro fertilization and have fertilized eggs tested for the CF gene before being implanted—only a fertilized egg unaffected by CF will be used, so the child will be safe from the disease
◆ to use donated sperm or eggs from a donor without a CF gene
◆ to conceive normally, but have a test during pregnancy
◆ to run the risk that their child could have CF, and not take a test or find out in advance.

After testing

If the parents have the pregnancy tested, they will then need to decide whether to have the baby aborted if it does have CF. Even if the baby has CF, it isn't possible to tell how badly it will be affected. If it doesn't have CF, there's still a chance it won't be

A simple test such as an oral swab can tell you whether you carry a gene defect that could cause CF.

healthy as there are many other disorders that aren't tested for. And even if a baby seems healthy when tested, it's possible that a gene could mutate (go wrong) later in his or her life. Many cancers are caused by gene mutations that occur long after birth.

Ask yourself

◆ If a woman knows the child she is carrying has CF, should she be allowed to abort it and try for a healthy baby?
◆ Is her right to an able-bodied child greater than the unborn child's right to be born? Who should decide?

The abortion debate

In some countries, abortion is illegal, and some religions—such as Catholicism—forbid it. Where abortion is allowed, some people object to it in all circumstances and would have no difficulty in deciding not to have an affected child aborted. Others may keep the child and hope that it would not be badly affected, or that treatment would be developed in time to cure it.

Many people think that if a child will suffer greatly or have a very poor quality of life, abortion may be the kindest choice. But as testing becomes more thorough, there will be difficult questions to address about how severe a condition should be before abortion will be allowed.

Opinions about whether abortion should be allowed often depend on when people believe life begins. At conception? When the egg can no longer split to form twins? When the brain develops? When the child could survive outside the womb?

Abortion stops a beating heart

In the U.K., abortion is allowed until the fetus is 24 weeks old. After this time, the child would stand a chance of survival if it was born. In the U.S., most states allow abortion up to 20 or 21 weeks.

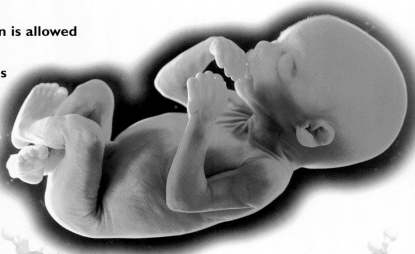

Gene therapy

At the moment, if tests show that a child has a defect, parents can be offered an abortion but not a chance to "mend" their child. With gene therapy, we'll be able to fix genetic problems either before a baby is born or in later life. Gene therapy involves implanting into someone's body a gene that they don't have or that, in their case, isn't working properly. It's likely that in the future people will be encouraged to undergo tests and have their child treated if there's anything wrong.

Stephen Hawking is a brilliant and influential physicist, yet he is completely disabled by amyotrophic lateral sclerosis, a condition that means he can't control his muscles. With genetic testing, how many exceptional people might never be born?

Ask yourself

◆ Should people be allowed to—or made to—test their unborn children?
◆ Should they have gene therapy for their baby if it is affected by something that can be corrected?
◆ Suppose a child will suffer from a condition that's uncomfortable or disfiguring, but not dangerous or painful. Should that be fixed?

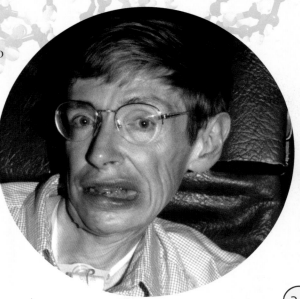

Choosing traits

Understanding genetics can give us the chance to make choices about the children we want to have. This could go beyond the choice to have a child free from a disabling or fatal condition. We might start to choose other, less important, features. Already, people can choose in some cases to have a boy or a girl. We'll soon have the information we need to choose whether to have a child with, say, blue eyes or great sporting skills.

Ask yourself

◆ Should we be allowed to choose the gender of our children?
◆ Should a couple with four boys be allowed to opt for a female fifth child?
◆ If a couple whose son was killed in an accident want their next child to be a boy too, should they have the choice?
◆ In a country in which the royal family's line may only continue through a male child, should the king and queen be allowed to choose to have a boy?

Boy or girl?

If a child is at risk of inheriting a disease that affects only boys or only girls, the parents may be allowed either to have the pregnancy ended if the child is of the "wrong" gender or, using IVF, have only fertilized eggs of the "right" gender put back into the mother's womb. Some people feel that interfering with nature in this way is wrong. But others argue that it would be wrong not to correct a disorder, given the chance.

Every parent wants a baby that will be intelligent, healthy, honest and talented. But should we engineer our children?

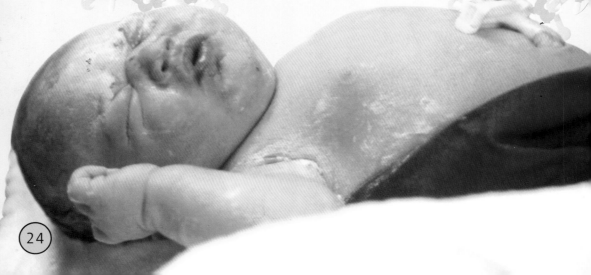

Eugenics

Eugenics is the attempt to improve the human race by getting rid of traits considered undesirable by the people in power. In the early 20th century in the U.S., many criminals, homosexuals, and mentally ill people were forcibly sterilized so that they couldn't have children and pass on their genes. The idea was to create a "purer" race. This was taken to extremes in the 1930s and '40s in Nazi Germany. Millions of Jews, mentally and physically disabled people, and homosexuals were killed as Hitler wanted a race of strong, blond, tall "Aryan" Germans.

Nowadays, few governments would openly kill or sterilize people in this way. But we can impose our ideas of genetic perfection by other means. If we prevent the birth of people with disabilities, or remove genes for certain types of behavior, we begin to create a society of people with chosen, preferred characteristics.

Eugenics led to some of the worst crimes of the 20th century, such as the mass extermination of Jews by the Nazis during World War II.

Ask yourself

◆ If we found a gene that made someone likely to become a child abuser or mass murderer, should we screen for it and not allow people to be born with that gene?

◆ What if parents refused to have their baby tested, or to have an affected baby genetically changed?

◆ Who would choose which traits we want people to have and which to avoid?

Choosing traits

Genetic engineering

Genetic engineering offers two ways of producing a baby with chosen characteristics:

◆ by fertilizing eggs outside the mother's body (IVF) and testing for the gene that's wanted or not wanted. Only eggs that match what the parents want are put back into the mother's womb.

◆ by testing the embryo inside the mother's womb or the fertilised egg outside the body and adding a changed gene to alter the baby's genetic make-up.

So far, only the first of these methods has been tried and tested.

Running a risk

Many genes act together. We don't understand how they do this, and it's likely that we'll know how to change individual genes before we understand how they work together with other genes. It could be dangerous to "repair" one gene without knowing what effect this might have on other genes, and hence on the developing baby. There may be a chance that by fixing one genetic defect we'd create another.

Case study

Molly Nash had a rare, fatal disease (Fanconi anemia) and could only be helped by a bone marrow transplant. A compatible donor couldn't be found, so her parents chose to have a second child whose bone marrow would match hers. Through IVF, doctors found an embryo that did not carry the disease and that would be a suitable donor. When Adam, her brother, was born, Molly was saved by a transfusion of blood from his umbilical cord. But 20 healthy embryos were discarded because they didn't match Molly's needs.

> *"Is it worse to be brought into the world to be a cord blood donor than not to exist at all? Because that's the choice... But for the fact he was a match for his sister, Adam Nash wouldn't exist".*
>
> JEFFREY KAHN, BIOETHICIST, UNIVERSITY OF MINNESOTA

Cloning

A clone is an exact genetic copy of a plant or animal. It is made by taking DNA from a single "parent" cell and putting it into an egg cell to grow. The first large animal to be cloned was Dolly the sheep, created in Scotland in 1997. She died in 2003 due to problems usually found in much older sheep. Premature aging is common in cloned animals.

Cloning might enable us to grow food without plants or animals—chicken nuggets from cloned chicken cells, for example. It could help us to create materials such as wood and rubber without having to wait for them to grow. We may also be able to produce cloned human tissue for use in organ transplants or skin grafts. Experimenting with human cloning is illegal in some countries. In others, some trials are allowed.

Ask yourself

◆ If you'd been genetically engineered, or cloned, how would you feel about it?
◆ Would it matter how and why you had been selected, created or changed?
◆ How would you feel if you had a genetic disorder and you found out that your parents had refused a test or genetic treatment that could have prevented your condition?

Dr Severino Antinori, an Italian doctor based in Rome, claims to be working on cloning a human baby. This has sparked a lot of media attention and public concern.

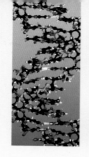

Finding out your fate

It's already possible to test people for some inherited conditions, and soon we'll be able to test for many more. But knowing how we're going to die may not be what we all want.

Looking into the future

Huntington's chorea is an inherited condition that's always fatal. The gene for it is dominant, so if one of your parents has Huntington's chorea, you have a 50 percent chance of having it yourself. Symptoms begin to appear in middle age. Until recently, someone with a parent who developed Huntington's chorea would have to wait and see if they had it too, but now it's possible to test for it and find out in advance.

Not knowing is stressful, but for some people knowing may be more stressful. Many people who have genetic tests like this need a lot of help in the form of counseling and advice to deal with their feelings, both before and after they know the result. This help isn't always available, so testing may lead them into an unbearable situation, perhaps worse than the uncertainty they had suffered before.

The issue is more complicated than it looks at first. If you found you didn't have the disease, you might feel guilty if it turned out that your brother or sister did have it.

Would you want to know how you're going to die? How would your friends and family react if you discovered you were developing an inherited disease?

Ask yourself

◆ If you knew you were going to die in middle age, would you plan your life and make the most of your time— or would you find it hard to cope?
◆ Perhaps you'd rather not know and try to live a "normal" life?

Taking control

Many cases are less clear-cut than Huntington's chorea. If you were found to have a gene that meant you were likely to develop a particular cancer or heart disease, there may be lots you could do to avoid it. You might be able to choose a healthy diet, take lots of exercise, or use preventive medicines to help you.

You may feel resentment and anger at your fate—or guilt if you don't live a healthy lifestyle to avoid problems. But even if you act on the knowledge, there's no guarantee you won't fall ill with something else that hasn't been predicted, or die from an accident.

Who cares?

Knowing that you may develop a particular genetic condition isn't of interest just to you. As a child, your family and school will also be affected. If you're an adult, your

The results of genetic testing can be devastating. The knowledge that someone will develop a condition that's hard to treat could cost them their job and their home.

employer, insurance company, and family will be involved. If an employer finds out that someone may take lots of time off sick in the future, the person may lose their job or be given fewer chances in their career. In a country that doesn't have free medical care for all, such as the U.S., people may not be able to get medical insurance if it's known that they might develop a condition that's expensive to treat. Even in a country where healthcare is free, such as the U.K., someone in this position may still lose their job, experience stress at home, or be unable to get a mortgage to buy a house or flat.

Finding out your fate

Sense of self

We all like to feel that we have some control over our lives and what we do. When situations such as poverty rob people of this control, they suffer stress and misery. If someone knew they were developing a disease they couldn't prevent or cure, would the consequences be the same? Knowing what is likely to happen to our health could deeply affect how we think of ourselves as free beings.

Economics

For society as a whole, however, it can be very useful to know what lies ahead. It may help governments plan healthcare and finances. And if we know someone is at risk, we may be able to save on expensive care later by teaching them to live healthily, or giving them preventive treatment.

Ask yourself

◆ Should we make people take tests to help plan future healthcare provision?
◆ Is it fair to make individuals do this for the benefit of society?
◆ Should someone who has been tested have to reveal the results of their tests to anyone else? If so, to whom?

Scientists can learn a lot from a blood sample. But genetic tests don't just affect the person tested. They can also have a knock-on effect on society as a whole.

Average life expectancy in the U.K.

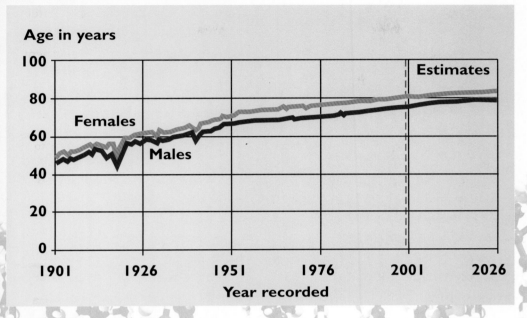

Age in years

Estimates

Females

Males

100
80
60
40
20
0

1901   1926   1951   1976   2001   2026

Year recorded

Longer life

If we worked out how to cure or prevent diseases that are common killers, people would live longer. This would have a serious impact on society, as old people generally don't work and so aren't making wealth for the country as a whole. Old people also need more healthcare resources than young people, as they are more prone to illness, slower to recover, and more likely to suffer serious consequences if they have an accident.

If genetics led to a rapidly aging population, the way society earns and spends money would need to change. Young people would need to plan pensions and take more

The average life expectancy of the population is rising, as shown in the diagram above. But fixing genetic problems could raise it even more. How would we cope?

responsibility for their futures than ever before. Those who earn may also have to pay more in taxes, or provide for the elderly in other ways.

Ask yourself

◆ Is it good for society or individuals to help people live longer and longer?
◆ Should we just accept that it is natural to grow old and die?
◆ What about the costs of caring for an aging population? Would we want to make the financial changes required?

Food for thought

Genetic research is as active in farming and food production as it is in human healthcare and medicine. You might have heard about GM (genetically modified) food, or GMOs (genetically modified organisms). It's an area where there's a lot of public concern and debate.

Genetic modification

A genetically modified organism (plant or animal) is made by adding a gene from one organism to another organism to give it a characteristic that's wanted. The gene can be from a completely different species—a gene from a moth can be added to a potato, for example. Each gene controls a characteristic. So if the moth can do something that would be useful in a potato—such as giving it resistance to disease—the gene that enables the moth to do it would be copied into the potato.

Is the oil seed rape in this field genetically modified or natural? It's impossible to tell. GM crops look the same as non-GM crops. Should we be told if they are grown near us?

GM foods

GM foods contain products from genetically modified plants. The GM crop may be the only ingredient, or it may be mixed with other, non-GM ingredients. There are several reasons for genetically modifying plants.

Some GM crops have a gene to make them resistant to a strong weed killer. Farmers can spray these crops with a chemical that will kill all the weeds in the field but won't harm the crop. They have to buy the seed and its tailor-made weed killer. This may cost more than other weed killers, but it's the only one they need.

Other GM crops have a gene that makes them produce a poison to protect them from a pest, such as a particular type of worm, beetle, moth, or fungus. The farmer then doesn't need a chemical pesticide.

Other changes can make plants resistant to frost, salty soil, disease, or drought, or give the product a longer shelf life after harvesting.

Concern

There has been little testing of genetically modified foods and some people think that they shouldn't be grown and eaten until we have researched what effects—if any— they have on people who eat them.

Ask yourself

- ◆ Should we be given proof that GM foods are safe before they go on sale, even though this research may take many years?
- ◆ Or should we take a chance, given that life is already full of health risks?
- ◆ Who should make the decision?

Those in favor

People who want to develop GM foods say that they will be useful because:

- ◆ they will help us to feed the world's growing population. GM crops can be developed to grow in land that can't be used at the moment because of unsuitable weather or soil conditions. GM crops can also be resistant to disease, weeds and pests
- ◆ GM foods can be developed to last longer in the shops without going bad
- ◆ GM animals and crops can be more productive—dairy cattle may give more milk, beef cattle may grow larger, plants may bear more fruit
- ◆ GM foods can be developed to have a higher nutritional value, so helping people to stay healthy.

33

Those against

People who are against GM foods offer these arguments:

◆ we don't know the final effects of what we are doing—it may be dangerous and could lead to a full-scale ecological disaster if changing genes produces unexpected side effects

◆ plant pollen is carried by the wind—it will be impossible to stop cross-pollination with plants in the wild and GM plants may wipe out some wild plants. Or we may end up with "super weeds" that are immune to weed killers thanks to a gene from GM crops

◆ there is no shortage of food in the world—political problems, distribution difficulties, and poverty are what stops the food getting to people who need it

◆ foods that last longer may end up with less nutritional value

◆ crops that are more productive and foods that last longer make money for food producers and shops, but no one else. We should not take risks to allow a few people to make money.

The developing world

GM crops still can't be grown for sale in the U.K., but many are being sold in the U.S. and to farmers in poorer countries. One of the claims for GM crops is that they will help to feed the world's poor—but not everyone is happy with this argument. The Ethiopian government banned GM crops in Ethiopia in

In many countries, there is public hostility towards the development of GM foods. This man is pulling up GM crops in protest.

Case study

New Leaf Superior is a GM potato developed by U.S. food company Monsanto. It is registered with the U.S. Environmental Protection Agency (EPA) as a pesticide because it has a gene which produces a poison to kill the Colorado potato beetle. This poison, called Bt, is listed by EPA as dangerous to inhale or get into wounds. But food labeling doesn't point this out—the company responsible for food labeling isn't allowed to label pesticides. Should food packaging contain information to help us make decisions about what we eat?

Will GM bring wealth to farmers and food to populations in poorer nations—or will it bring economic dependence and famine?

1999, saying that poverty was the reason for their country's hunger, not that they couldn't grow enough food. The government objected to the use of Ethiopia's poverty to change opinions about GM foods in Europe.

Suicidal seeds

Developing GM crops is expensive and the companies that produce them don't want farmers to be able to get more seeds without paying. One way of avoiding this happening is to add "terminator genes"—genes that stop the crop producing seeds that will grow. This is sometimes called gene

protection (GP). It also prevents seeds from GM plants accidentally escaping into the wild. Farmers in poorer countries, who traditionally save seeds from year to year, may suffer most if terminator genes take off. India has already banned GP.

Ask yourself

◆ Are we using poorer countries to test GM crops we won't use ourselves?
◆ Are large corporations risking the livelihood of farmers in poorer parts of the world?

Food for thought

Who is eating GM foods?

Although there's no agreement yet on GM foods, already 25 percent of corn grown in the U.S. is genetically modified. GM foods and ingredients don't have to be labelled in the U.S. as they are considered no different from non-GM foods. GM soya, for example, is mixed with non-GM soya before going on sale, unlabeled. In the U.K., GM tomato puree is sold without marking on the label.

This lack of knowledge makes people worry that their food is no longer what they think it is. Many are concerned about what they are eating—that a tomato with a fish gene is no longer a true tomato, for example.

The gene that keeps this young flounder from freezing in very cold seas could help us to grow tomatoes that are resistant to frost. Could genes like this solve harvesting problems in the future?

Ask yourself

◆ Is a vegetable with an animal gene still a pure vegetable? How would a vegetarian see it?
◆ If a vegetable had a gene originally derived from humans, would it make you a cannibal if you ate the vegetable? Or is a gene just a chemical anyway?
◆ Is it right to mix up genes from different species—to form transgenic creatures?

Not just food

As well as modifying foods for improved production, genetic engineers are also working on other ideas. These include:

◆ bananas grown to give protection against diseases— instead of vaccinating people in poorer nations, scientists are trying to develop bananas containing drugs, so that eating the fruit will give people the necessary immunity

◆ a protein-enriched GM potato that the Indian government intends to give to underfed children who don't usually get enough protein in their diet

◆ silkworms that produce a very strong thread, much stronger than normal silk

◆ cows whose milk is very similar to human breast milk, so that women who can't breastfeed their babies have a better alternative

◆ plants that produce a type of plastic in their leaves so that we don't need to extract and process oil to make plastics

◆ mosquitoes that can't carry malaria—scientists aim to replace malaria-carrying mosquitoes with GM ones, in the hope of one day eliminating a disease that kills millions of people every year

Ask yourself

◆ Is it right to alter a plant or animal's genes for our own purposes?
◆ Is it safe to make changes to the genes of other animals or plants when we don't know what the results may be, either for the other organism or for us?
◆ Is it fair to kill off a whole species, even if it is harmful to humans?

Scientists hope eventually to kill most of the naturally occurring mosquitoes in a malarial area and release new GM mosquitoes to take over.

Made for you

With genetic engineering, scientists aim to make things that we, as humans, need. These may be medicines or food or organs for transplant. Do we mind how these things are created?

Micro factories

We are already using bacteria as tiny "factories" to make chemicals for us. People with diabetes have difficulty processing sugar in their bodies. To keep them healthy, they need frequent injections of insulin. This used to be taken from pigs, but geneticists have now found a gene that makes human insulin and have put it into bacteria. The bacteria are grown in large vats and the insulin they produce is taken out and used for diabetic treatments.

Eat dirt!

Pollution is one of the main problems faced by our planet. Yet there are some bacteria and plants that can break down some of the chemicals that cause pollution, and leave harmless chemicals in their place. To use them would mean releasing GMOs into the environment to spread. This is just what we are trying not to do with GM crops.

Ask yourself

◆ Do you approve of moves to clean up pollution by using GMOs?
◆ Do you think the potential benefit—cleaning up pollution—justifies the risk of releasing GMOs into the wild?
◆ Might we become more careless of how we treat our planet if we can easily clear up any mess with the help of GMOs?

Human insulin can be produced by bacteria, and soon scientists may also be able to grow it in sheep's milk or eggs.

Grow your own

Scientists are also experimenting with growing new tissue from human stem cells. Stem cells are the cells that make up an embryo before it starts to develop different body parts. These cells have the ability to grow into anything—skin, bone, blood, or muscle. It's possible that they could be used to grow tissue for skin grafts, and blood or bone marrow for transfusion. But research with stem cells so far means using "spare" human embryos produced during IVF treatment. Some people don't approve of this.

Pig hearted

Equally controversial is research into organ transplants. As doctors have become more successful at carrying out transplants, we have reached the point where there are not enough organs—hearts, kidneys, livers etc— for all the people who need them.

Geneticists are now developing pigs with hearts that could be used in human transplants. This would enable surgeons to carry out many more transplants, but some people worry that it might introduce new diseases to people. It might also be traumatic for people to have organs taken from animals, perhaps affecting their view of how "human" they are.

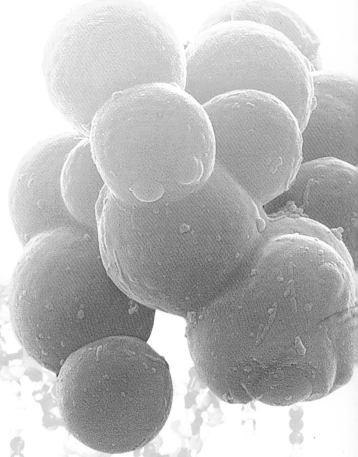

A fertilized egg could grow into a baby—or a patch of skin for skin grafts. There's disagreement over whether it is acceptable to use "spare" IVF embryos—which could, if used differently, grow into people—for genetic research.

Ask yourself

◆ Is it right to create animals to use for spare parts or to modify them to produce medicines? Is it any different from using animals for food?
◆ If you needed a transplant, would you rather have an organ from an animal or risk a long wait for a human donor?

Ends and means

Y̶ou might have found as you read the previous chapters of this book that you were asking yourself similar questions again and again. In this chapter, we will sum up some of the issues that keep coming up as we think about genetics.

Should we meddle with nature?

The world around us is the product of billions of years of evolution. Animals and plants have developed slowly, adapting as the world has changed. Unsuccessful species have died out, and species that are well suited to the conditions in which they live have flourished.

Now that we are able to alter the genetic make-up of plants and animals—and even of ourselves— we can make very rapid changes. Some are changes that might have occurred eventually anyway—but most would probably never have happened. We can't know if we are causing any damage by doing this and it may be decades before we see the consequences of some of our actions. Some people believe that we shouldn't meddle with nature in this way.

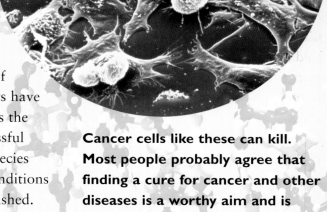

Cancer cells like these can kill. Most people probably agree that finding a cure for cancer and other diseases is a worthy aim and is helped by genetic research.

Others believe that we should do all we can to try to conquer disease and famine and that genetics offers us valuable chances to do this.

Ask yourself

◆ What do you think? Do the ends—a cure for cancer, food for the starving— justify the means, whatever they may be?
◆ Or are we risking the whole planet in a dangerous experiment?

Do animals have rights?

A growth hormone called bovine sematotrophin (BST) is often given to cattle to make them produce more milk. It used to be taken from the brains of dead cows, but is now made by GM bacteria. The problem is, the new BST seems to be bad for cows. It makes them more likely to fall ill and develop ulcers that won't heal. To counter this, they are fed a lot of antibiotics. Is this fair practice?

What is "safe?"

Milk from cows that have been given genetically engineered BST can't be sold in the EU because of possible risks to human health. But farmers in the US are allowed to sell it and the milk doesn't have to be labeled as coming from treated cows. They say it's safe. Whose definition of "safe" can we believe?

Case study

In 1956, Brazilian farmers imported a strain of aggressive bees from Africa as they wanted to breed better honeybees. Their experiment went wrong (some of the bees escaped) and now parts of North and South America are plagued by swarms of killer bees that have caused over 1000 deaths. Is there a chance that genetic trials could fail like this?

Do we have the right to give cows a genetically engineered hormone that benefits ourselves but harms the animals? Would you drink milk that you knew had come from treated cows?

Ends and means

Who has a say?

We share the world with people who have a wide range of views—and all people in every country could be affected by developments in genetics.

The Inuit tribe believe that all animals are worthy of equal respect. A member of the Jain religion will not harm any living creature. Changing animals genetically for our own means would probably seem unacceptable to these people. You may or may not share these views—but as many of these people are from poorer nations, their voices are unlikely to be heard.

The Inuit, from northern Canada, depend on local wildlife for their livelihood. How would they feel about genetic trials on animals?

Ask yourself

◆ Who should decide whose views count on global matters, such as what we do with our world and with our genes?
◆ Does the president of a global biotech corporation have more right to be heard than a tribesman in an Afghan village? If so, why?

Bringing back the dead

As we learn more about how our genes work, and as genetic processes become cheaper, all kinds of things will become possible.

One day we may be able to recreate extinct creatures. In 2002, Australian scientists made public their plans to "make" a Tasmanian tiger (which has been extinct for over 60 years) from fragments of DNA.

Could genetic cloning bring back the dodo?

We might eventually be able to clone a dead pet. If your dog died, you could re-create it (though it wouldn't be identical as factors other than genes will affect how it develops). And one day we may even be able to clone humans. How would our attitude towards life change if cloning became common?

"Seven mammalian species have now been cloned. Very few clones survive... The lucky ones die early. The ones who survive are unlucky because the prediction is that they will be abnormal. To argue humans might be different... ignores all scientific evidence."

RUDOLF JAENISCH, PROFESSOR OF BIOLOGY, MASSACHUSSETTS INSTITUTE OF TECHNOLOGY, 2002

New creations

Perhaps we could even keep a bank of DNA of all species so that we could create them at will, or use their DNA for other purposes. Maybe we could make new creatures. If a movie needed a dragon, at some point in the future we might be able to make one. So far, the possibilities are unknown.

Could genetic engineering spell the end of special effects in films? How long before you can have a pet dragon, or a real Neopet?

Ask yourself

◆ Should we bring back animals we've destroyed in the past? Would it make us less careful of existing rare species?
◆ What about animals that became extinct naturally? Would it be fair to test their ability to survive all over again?

Who cares?

Who's looking after our interests? Research into genetics is carefully watched by ethics committees, but legislation (law-making) can't always keep up with the fast pace of scientific advances. Can we make a difference as members of the public?

Ethics committees

Ethics committees are groups of people who meet to discuss the work carried out by scientists in research institutions and hospitals. An ethics committee tries to represent the views of everyone who will have an interest in an issue and make decisions about

Some of the people on an ethics committee are subject experts, while others are philosophers with an interest in ethics or morals.

what is wrong and what is right. They discuss individual cases and more abstract issues. An ethics committee in a hospital might discuss the case of an individual patient. Or an ethics committee might be appointed by the government to discuss whether research into a particular area should be allowed.

The Human Genome Project was the first large-scale scientific project to look closely at the ethical, legal, and social issues raised by its work. Other scientific projects have left this for different groups to consider.

The law

Each country may draw up its own laws, and in some areas of research these can differ considerably. At the moment, some procedures are legal in some places but not in others.

Laws made here in the European Parliament may conflict with laws made elsewhere. Is this fair? If something is allowed in Europe, but not in the U.S., should you be able to travel to do or get it?

Vested interests

Many of the people working in controversial fields like genetics have a vested interest—they may be trying to make money, or further their own careers. But in a specialized area, they are the people who know most about the issues. How they explain things can make a huge difference to society because our opinions depend on the information they supply. We need to be sure we are basing our views on balanced facts and not on biased arguments.

Case study

Surrogate motherhood—when a woman carries embryos for another woman and hands over the baby after birth—is illegal in Italy but allowed in the U.S.. After an Italian woman paid an American woman and airmailed frozen twin embryos to her, the Italian health minister planned to make "embryo tourism" illegal. Italy is a Catholic country, and many Catholics believe that life starts at the moment of conception and must not be interfered with. But not everyone in Italy is a Catholic.

"It is unacceptable that a religious viewpoint should become that of the State."

GIOVANNI MAPELLI, CENTRE FOR THEOLOGICAL STUDIES, MILAN

Ask yourself

Who do you think we can trust to:
◆ know enough about the science and issues concerned?
◆ put the interests of all sectors of society first?

Your own opinion

By now you should have enough background knowledge to start to form your own views on genetics. These may be the same as or different from your friends. But keep asking questions and finding things out. Try to understand all sides of the story. The more you learn, the stronger your arguments will be.

Further work

Listed here are some useful resources that will help you find out more about genetics.

http://ehrweb.aaas.org/ehr/books/contents.html (html)
or http://ehrweb.aaas.org/ehr/books/yourgenes (pdf: printable version)
Your genes, your choices
A guide intended for the general public. It helps to explain genetics and discusses the choices that advances in genetic engineering are giving us.

www.ornl.gov/hgmis/
The official website of the Human Genome Project.

Brave New World
Aldous Huxley, 1932
A novel about the future. Huxley imagines a world in which all babies are grown outside the human body. They are genetically engineered on a scale from very intelligent to mentally subnormal so that they are "made" for specific jobs and social functions.

Genetic Engineering: The Facts
Sally Morgan, Evans Brothers Limited, 2001
A great book introducing the science behind genetic engineering.

What's the Big Idea? Genetics
Martin Brookes, Hodder Children's Books, 1998
An easy-to-understand book about how we inherit characteristics and how our genes work.

Gattaca
Andrew Niccol, 1997
A movie set in the future in which everyone is ruled by their genetic code and babies are engineered. Everyone's fate is known from birth and people can have each other genetically tested anonymously. Anyone not genetically engineered is an "in-valid" and has a low status in society.

Time to act!

If you feel strongly about any of the issues raised in this book, take action. Write to your local supermarket to find out about its policy on GM foods. Contact local farmers or your representative in parliament with your views. If you want to join a campaign or sign a petition, contact an environmental group. If you want to find out more about research into genetics or the biotechnology business, start at the website of the Human Genome Project (www.ornl.gov/hgmis/) and follow links to different areas.

Glossary

chromosome A complete molecule of DNA. Chromosomes carry genetic information. They are present in all biological cells and copy themselves when new cells grow.

clone An exact genetic copy of a single plant or animal.

cross-pollination Pollinating one type or group of plants with pollen from another.

DNA Deoxyribonucleic acid —a complex chemical which forms long, string-like molecules. Chromosomes are made up of DNA.

dominant (gene) A gene that will always be expressed— the characteristic it relates to will develop—if you inherit it from one of your parents.

donor A person who gives body tissue or parts to be used by someone else—a sperm donor gives sperm that may be used to father a child, a blood donor gives blood for transfusion, and so on.

embryo The early stage of a developing baby. In humans, a baby is called an embryo from the second to the eighth week of pregnancy.

fetus A developing baby after its main body parts have formed. In humans, the baby is called a fetus from the ninth week of pregnancy until birth.

genetic disorder An illness or disability caused by a problem with genes.

genetic engineering Working with genes to make changes to a plant or animal.

genetically-modified organism A plant or animal that has been changed by altering its genes—adding genes from another type of plant or animal, for example.

immune Protected from a disease or condition.

inherit In this context, to gain a characteristic from a parent through their genes.

in vitro fertilisation (IVF) Fertilizing an egg outside the mother's body.

patent Legal recognition that someone thought of and/or owns an invention.

pesticide A chemical that is used to kill a pest, such as a fungus or an insect that destroys a crop.

recessive (gene) A gene that will only be expressed—the characteristic it relates to will develop—if you inherit two copies of it, one from each parent.

species A group of plants or animals that are similar in most ways and can therefore interbreed.

strain A particular variety of plant or animal.

transplant An operation in which surgeons replace an organ that's not working properly with a healthy organ from another person or from an animal.

47

Index